THE SUPER SCIENCE BOOK OF
ROCKS AND SOILS

Robert Snedden

Rest

Under cool, black bobbles of earth
Grey-ringed worms wind round brown-skinned bulbs,
Burrowing moles push buried bones aside
And sleeping seeds awake and stretch,
While ancient coins lie bitten and bent
And cat's lost tooth sits white and sharp.

Secret treasures dangling in a
Shipwreck of tangly roots,
Laid to rest in earth.

Rocks sit stock still,
Worlds within worlds
Of permanent suspension.
Locked inside a granite tomb, an amber chunk
Clasps a bee in flight
And a spiraled ammonite
Is stuck circling for thousands of years.
But through the thinnest crack a creature scuttles –
An arrested crab is caught
In the glare of the midday sun.

by Lizzie Lewis

Illustrations by Frances Lloyd

Thomson Learning • New York

Books in the Super Science series

Energy	**Our Bodies**
The Environment	**Rocks and Soils**
Forces	**Sound**
Life Processes	**Space**
Light	**Time**
Materials	**Weather**

First published in the
United States in 1995 by
Thomson Learning
115 Fifth Avenue
New York, NY 10003

First published in Great Britain in 1994 by
Wayland (Publishers) Ltd.

Library of Congress Cataloging-in-Publication Data
Snedden, Robert.
  The super science book of rocks and soils / Robert
Snedden; illustrations by Frances Lloyd.
      p.   cm. – (Super science)
  Includes bibliographic references and index.
  ISBN 1-56847-224-2
  1. Geology – Juvenile literature. 2. Soils – Juvenile
literature. [1. Rocks. 2. Soils. 3. Geology.] I. Lloyd,
Frances, ill. II. Title. III. Series.
QE29.S65   1995
552 – dc20   94-20897

Printed in Italy

Series Editor: Jim Kerr
Designer: Loraine Hayes Design

Picture acknowledgments

Illustrations by Frances Lloyd
Cover illustration by Martin Gordon

Photographs by permission of: de Beers 18 top; Eye
Ubiquitous 12 both, 21 top (P. Craven), 25 top (Judith Platt);
G.S.F. Picture Library 4, 5, 9 top and bottom, 15, 17, 22;
Natural History Museum 18 bottom; Still Pictures/Mark
Edwards 29; Science Photo Library 11 (David Weintraub), 16
(Jan Hinsch), 19 bottom (Sheila Terry), 21 bottom (Dr.
Jeremy Burgess); Tony Stone Worldwide 8 (Dennis Oda), 13
(Oliver Strewe), 23 (Steve Climpson), 28 (Jacques Jangoux);
Wayland Picture Library 25 bottom, 26; ZEFA 7.

CONTENTS

WHAT ARE ROCKS?

There are many different kinds of rocks. It is usual to think of rocks as being very hard and perhaps big as well, but there are some softer, smaller materials, such as sand, gravel, and clay, that are also rocks.

Every rock is made up of one or ▶ more different materials called minerals. Minerals themselves are made up of one or more different elements. Elements are made of only one substance. Oxygen, for example, contains only oxygen. When different elements combine with one another they form compounds. A mineral is any solid element or compound that is found naturally in the earth. Minerals are the building blocks from which the earth is made. For example, when the elements silicon and oxygen combine, they form a mineral called quartz. Quartz together with the minerals feldspar and mica make up the rock called granite, which is pictured here.

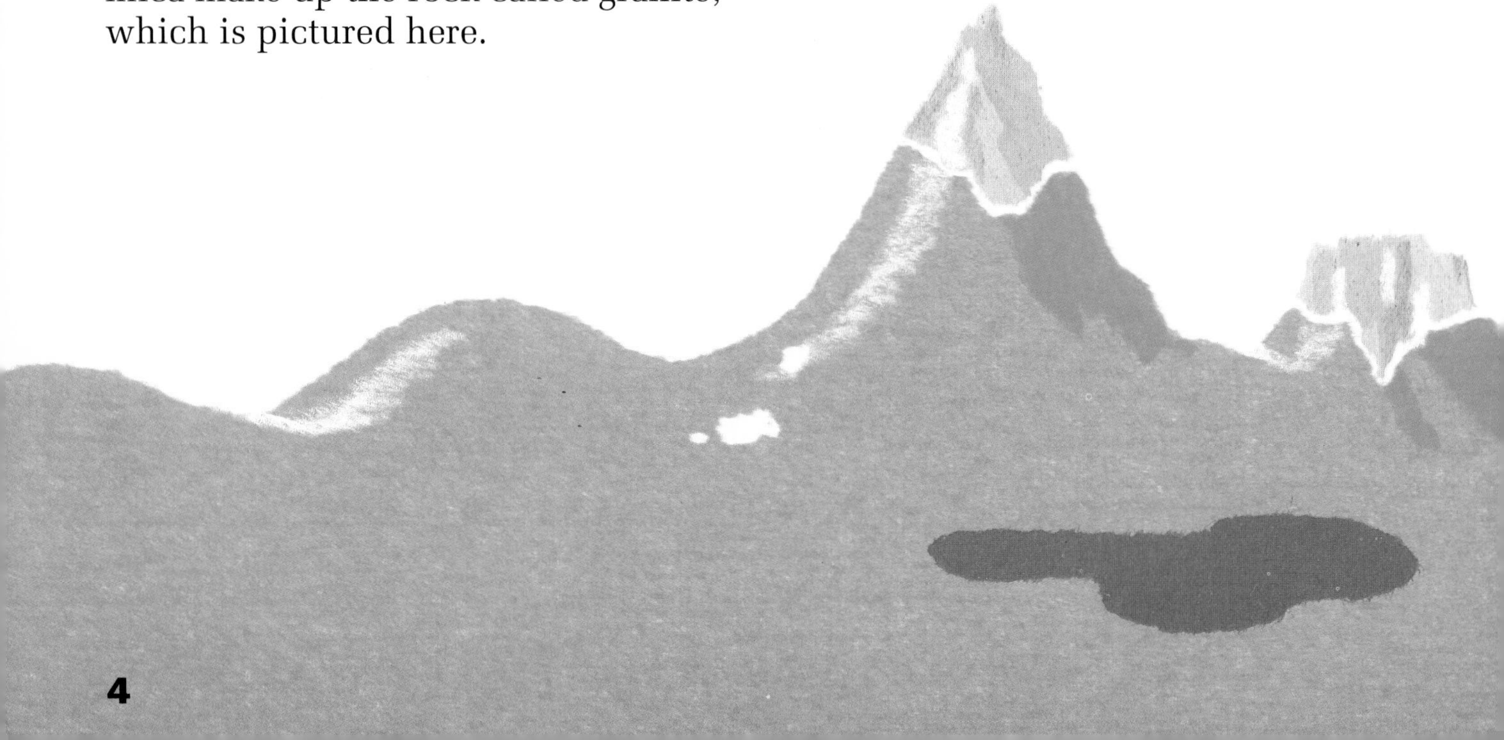

◀ Most minerals can be found as crystals. Crystals form when minerals that have been melted or dissolved become solid. The elements that make up the mineral form themselves into regular patterns. The more slowly this happens, the bigger the crystals that form.

Growing crystals

The process of forming a crystal is called crystallization.

1 Take some ordinary table salt – a very common mineral – and dissolve it a little at a time in some very warm water until no more salt dissolves.

2 Pour a little of the solution of salt and water into a shallow dish and put it to one side to cool. You may have to leave the dish for a day or two until the water evaporates completely.

Once the water has evaporated, you should find crystals of salt that are much bigger than those you dissolved in the water.

LOOKING INSIDE THE EARTH

Get a drinking glass and tap it ▶ gently with your finger. Listen to the sound it makes. Now fill it with water and tap it again. It will sound different. You can tell whether a glass is full or empty just by tapping it, even when your eyes are closed. If the earth were tapped, just like the glass, would it tell us what is inside?

Whole sections of the earth's surface are moving very, very slowly – far too slowly for anyone to see. As the sections move, rocks are being bent and pulled. Sometimes the rocks just can't bend anymore and they break apart suddenly. When this happens, a great deal of energy is released all at once. We call this an earthquake. ▼

Every time there is an earthquake, shock waves travel through the earth as if it were being tapped by a giant finger. By measuring the way these shock waves travel – what direction they go in and how long they take to reach other places – it has been possible to build up a picture of the inside of the earth.

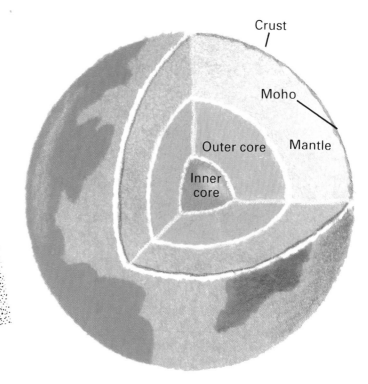

Crust

Moho

Outer core

Mantle

Inner core

WOW!
An earthquake in China in 1556 killed almost one million people.

▲ Earthquakes can be incredibly destructive. A powerful earthquake can flatten a whole city. The earthquake that damaged San Francisco in 1989 was only about one hundredth of the strength of a really big quake.

ROCK FORMATION

The outer part of the earth (on which we live) is called its crust. The crust is made up of three main types of rock. Each type is formed in a different way.

Igneous rocks are formed from molten material called magma that comes from deep inside the earth. Sometimes magma cools slowly under the surface, but sometimes it explodes from a volcano as lava. Igneous rocks are also called volcanic rocks. ▶

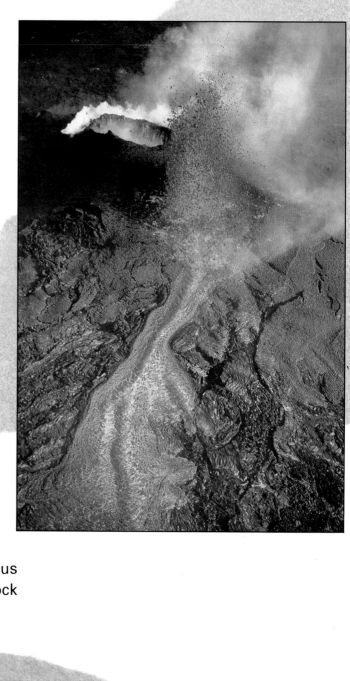

Igneous
rock

Sedimentary rocks are formed from ▶
the remains of older rocks that have
been worn away. Layer upon layer of
rock pieces may be gathered together
in one place by water, wind, ice, or as
sediments at the bottom of the sea.
Eventually, the weight of the layers
above presses the bottom layers
together so hard that they join together
into solid rock again. Rocks that form
beneath the sea may also contain
pieces of the shells of small animals.

◀ Metamorphic rocks are
rocks that have been
changed by fierce heat
or pressure inside the
earth, although they have
not melted. The elements
that make up the rocks
may be rearranged, but
no new ones are added
or old ones taken away.

At one time the whole of the earth's crust was formed
from igneous rocks. It has taken millions of years for
the other types of rocks to be formed. The changing
of rocks from one type to another, called the rock
cycle, is still going on.

Metamorphic rock

Sedimentary rock

WEATHERING AND EROSION

Sedimentary rocks are formed from worn-away pieces of other rocks. The breaking down of a rock is called weathering. Rocks can be worn down by changes of temperature. Rocks expand as they get hot and then shrink again as they cool down.

In places such as deserts where the days are very hot and the nights are cold, the constant expanding and contracting begins to break down the rock. Thin sheets start to peel away from its surface. This is called onion-skin weathering because of the appearance it gives the rock. ▶

◀ Rocks can be broken by ice. Water expands when it freezes. If water gets into a crack in a rock and then turns into ice, it pushes the crack open. When the ice melts, water can get farther into the rock so that when the water freezes again it opens the crack a bit more. Eventually the rock will break open altogether.

Rocks are also worn away by chemicals. Acid rain results when chemicals that are produced by burning fuels in power plants and car engines get into the atmosphere and mix with moisture. It then falls as acid rain, which attacks rocks. You can often see the damage caused to rocks that have been used in buildings or to ◀ make statues.

After a rock has been broken up, the pieces may be moved to a different place, perhaps by wind, water, or ice. This is called erosion. As the rock fragments are carried along they bump against one another. This breaks them down even more. Desert sand dunes are built up from tiny fragments of rocks that have been weathered by heat and cold and eroded by the wind. ▼

FOSSILS

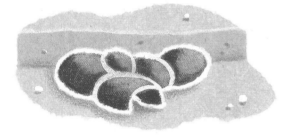

Formation of a fossil

Fossils are the traces left in rock of plants and animals that lived millions of years ago. A fossil can be a track left by an animal or the animal itself. Most fossils are found in sedimentary rocks. As the layers that will make up the sedimentary rock are laid down by erosion, the shells or skeletons of dead animals or the parts of a plant may be trapped between the layers. New minerals fill the spaces left by the creature once it has dissolved. Geologic time periods have been established by scientists based on the types of fossils found in rock and on evolutionary data.

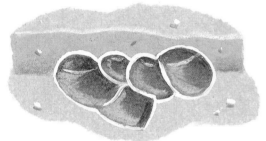

Dead animal remains are buried

Remains dissolve leaving
fossil mold

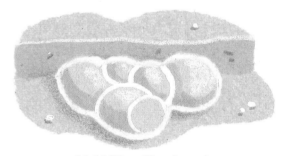

Mold fills with minerals
to form fossil cast

570 Million years ago	500 Million years ago	435 Million years ago	395 Million years ago	345 Million years ago
Cambrian	Ordovician	Silurian	Upper Devonian	Carboniferous

Make your own fossil
1 Put a layer of soft clay in a shallow container such as a frozen food tray. Find a shell or a twig and press it into the clay so that it leaves the outline of its shape.

2 Take your shell or twig away, then carefully pour plaster of paris into the space in the clay.

3 When the plaster is dry, remove it carefully. You should find that you have made a cast of your original specimen. A fossil of your shell or twig would look something like this.

Studying fossils helps us to discover what life was like on earth millions of years ago and how living things have changed to become the plants and animals we see around us today. By carefully studying the ways in which plants and animals have changed, it is possible to get some idea of the age of rocks from the fossils found in them. These bones are being uncovered at the Dinosaur National Monument in Colorado. They belonged to a dinosaur that lived on earth over 65 million years ago. ▶

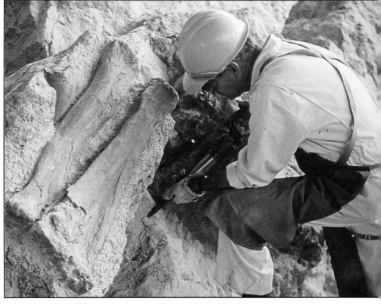

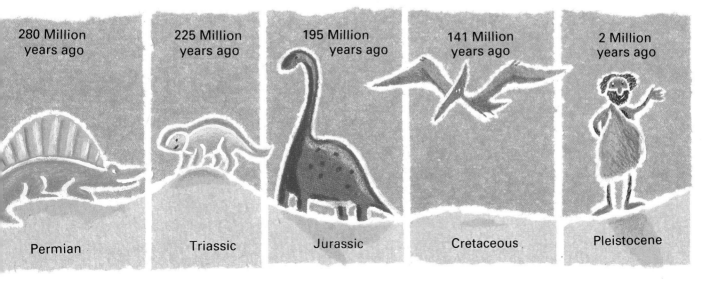

| 280 Million years ago | 225 Million years ago | 195 Million years ago | 141 Million years ago | 2 Million years ago |
| Permian | Triassic | Jurassic | Cretaceous | Pleistocene |

FOSSIL WEALTH

Some ancient plant ▶ and animal remains eventually become very valuable. Tiny organisms called plankton are found in the sea. When plankton die, they may sink to the bottom to become part of the sediment that forms on the seabed.

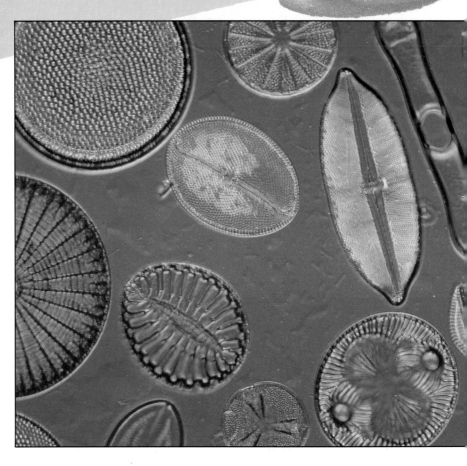

As the sediments build up and become sedimentary rock, the remains of the plankton are slowly changed. Over time, they decay to form the oil and gas we use today for fuel. These fuels are held in porous rocks, such as sandstone, which have many tiny spaces or holes. Above this is a layer of solid rock, called a cap rock, which traps the oil or gas in the rocks beneath it. The cap rock has to be drilled through to reach the oil.

Coal is also a type of sedimentary rock. It is formed from the remains of trees and other plants that lived billions of years ago. A coal bed can begin to form in damp, swampy areas where there are lots of plants growing. When the plants die, they are covered by layers of mud that squeeze and crush them. Over millions of years, as more layers of mud and sediment form on top, the plants slowly change into black coal.

OIL

In the eighteenth and nineteenth centuries, British farmers often used local rock to make stone walls to enclose their lands. It is often possible to tell where the types of rocks change between different areas by looking at the rocks used to make these walls. Even today, some people still learn the art of making walls from natural rock without using bricks or cement to hold the wall together.

In more recent times, brownstone buildings in New York City were built using sandstone, the color of which gives the buildings their name. The sandstone came from quarries along the Connecticut River about 65 miles away and from Scotland, brought over in the nineteenth century as ballast to give empty sailing ships extra weight so that they would float safely. ▼

▲ Stone fragments, called aggregates, are often used in the building industry. They are used to make foundations for building houses or roads or are mixed with cement to make concrete. To make the aggregate, rocks are dynamited from the land and then crushed at a quarry. In some places gravel – small, rounded stones that have been weathered and eroded by water – can be found. Gravel makes an excellent aggregate.

CAVING
AND CLIMBING

◄ Many people enjoy exploring the earth's rocks, both above the surface and beneath it. A deep underground cave is formed when limestone is weathered by water seeping into it. Over long periods of time, small openings in the rock become wider and wider as the water dissolves the limestone. Underground rivers and lakes can form. Water dripping from the roof of the cave can leave deposits of calcium carbonate, a mineral found in limestone. These deposits build up into stalactites, which hang from the roof of the cave. Other deposits build up on the floor of the cave to form stalagmites. Sometimes the stalactites and stalagmites join together to form continuous columns.

Some people like the challenge of climbing the cliffs and stacks that the sea carves from rocks along the coast. The power of the waves crashing against the shore causes the shore rocks to erode. Where the rocks are particularly weak, the water cuts sea caves into the cliffs. If two caves are formed back to back on a narrow headland, the sea may cut all the way through to form an arch. Often the top of the arch will collapse and a finger of rock, called a sea stack, remains, cut off from the shore. ▶

WOW!
The largest caves in the world are beneath the Mammoth Cave National Park in Kentucky. Over 300 miles of passageways have been found so far.

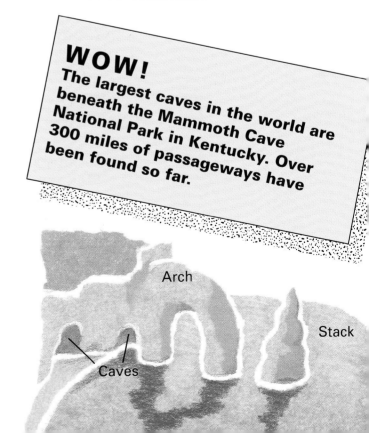

Arch

Stack

Caves

▲ Mountains are formed where the moving sections of the earth's surface crash into each other. The Himalayas, the largest mountain range on Earth, were formed when India collided with the rest of Asia about 40 million years ago. After the collision, India kept moving north for another 1,200 miles, pushing the mountains up as it went.

WOW!
India is still moving north at the rate of about half an inch per year.

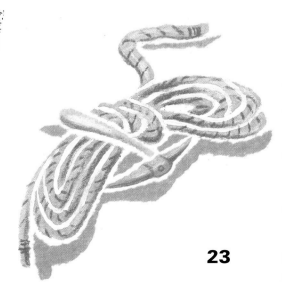

SOILS

Soil covers much of the earth's ▶ surface above the sea. In some places, such as the polar ice caps, there is no soil at all. In other places it may be many feet thick. Plants grow in soil, which provides the minerals they need to grow.

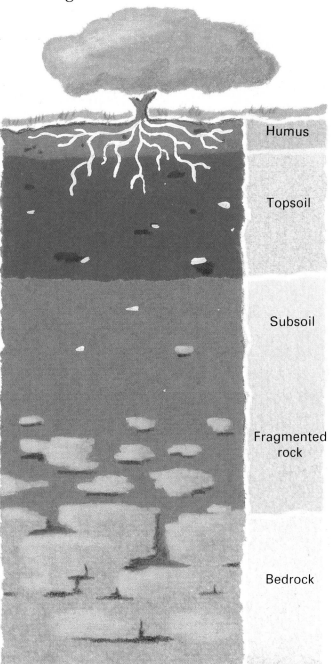

Humus

Topsoil

Subsoil

Fragmented rock

Bedrock

Weathering breaks down rock into smaller pieces, which may eventually become part of the soil. The type of soil depends on the rocky material from which it is made. Sandy soils, not surprisingly, come from sandstone, for example, but you might not guess that clay soils come from granite. Climate is important in the formation of soil, since rainfall and temperature changes affect how the rock is broken down.

◀ If you dug a deep hole through soil, you would see that it is made up of different layers. Each layer is called a horizon. Part of the top layer is made up of a mixture of minerals and humus, the decaying remains of plants and animals. The second layer, called topsoil, contains some minerals that have been washed down by the rain; it is in this layer that seeds germinate and grow. The third layer, or subsoil, containing weathered rock particles, lies on top of a layer of larger fragments of weathered rock. And the fragmented rock sits on top of the bedrock, the original rock on which the soil was formed.

◀ Tough living things such as lichens and mosses are the first to establish themselves on the rock surface. Their small size allows them to take advantage of cracks in the rock, where they can escape the extremes of temperature and dryness often found on bare rocks. Lichens produce acids that dissolve the rock, making it release its minerals and breaking it down even more. When the plants die, their remains become part of the soil that builds up over the rock.

As the soil gets ▶ deeper, larger plants can grow in it. It may take hundreds or even thousands of years to happen, but eventually, where before there was only bare rock, a forest may grow.

LEAF LITTER LIFE

Soil can hold a remarkable variety and number of living things. In a field, the weight of earthworms under the soil may be greater than the weight of the cattle above it!

Most of the soil creatures are ▶ decomposers. These animals digest and break down the waste and dead bodies of other animals and plants. By doing this they return minerals to the soil so that growing plants can use them again. The animals that live in woodland soil get most of their food from the leaves that fall from the trees. Some animals, like earthworms, eat the leaves and break them down into pieces that tiny insects and other small animals can eat. Spiders and beetles eat these smaller animals. Other animals may eat the fungi and bacteria that also feed on the leaves.

WOW!
There may be nearly 5,000 insects and mites living under one square foot of a field. An acre of one field in southern England had over 2 million spiders living on it.

Making a wormery

The earthworm plays a big part in maintaining the good health of the soil. You can watch earthworms at work by constructing a wormery. You will need to ask an adult to help with finding the materials and making this. You might suggest it as a school project.

2 Fill the frame with layers of different soils, such as garden soil, peat, and sand. Water it well.

1 Make a U-shaped, three-sided wooden frame about 20 inches square and 6 inches deep. Attach a sheet of strong, clear plastic to the front and back.

3 Place ten or twelve big worms on the top with some leaves and grass cuttings for food.

4 Cover the wormery with an old cloth to keep it dark.

In a few days the worms will have begun to mix up the different soil layers as they tunnel through them. You will be able to see their burrows. This is what happens naturally. The worms mix up the soil, introducing air into it and improving it by helping to break down the old plant material and put the minerals back into the soil. You might try putting different types of leaves on the surface of your wormery to see which ones the worms like best.

Remember to look after your worms. Keep them well fed and the soil moist. After all, you want to see how they behave naturally. When you've finished watching them, put them back where they came from.

SOILS AND FARMING

▲ A field of wheat or corn swaying in the breeze may look natural, but it isn't. Plants do not grow naturally in huge groups of only one type of plant. Normally, many different types of plants grow together. A field is artificial. It takes a huge amount of energy to maintain a field full of a crop such as potatoes or corn. Fuel is needed for the machinery used to plant the seed, to spray pesticides and fertilizer, and to harvest the crop when it is ripe.

As we have seen, when a plant dies it is broken down by living things in the soil so that the minerals it contains can be used again by the plants that come after it. In tropical rain forests the soils are actually very poor, but plant material is broken down and minerals are returned to it very quickly. In parts of the Amazon, local farmers cut down and burn small areas of rain forest. They farm the land for a short while and then move on to another area to let the rain forest grow back. This makes sure that the soil is not badly damaged.

◄ When large numbers of trees are destroyed to make way for grasslands to feed cattle, the poor soil can only support farming for a few years.

Perhaps the soil wouldn't really be lost forever. Eventually it might be found as a sediment at the bottom of the sea. Millions of years later it might form part of a sedimentary rock. And millions of years after *that* it might be broken down into soil again. By the time the rock cycle has gone that far around, who knows what strange plants might grow there!

▲ The roots of plants help to bind the soil together. If there were no plants, the soil would soon dry out or get washed away by heavy rain. New plants would not be able to grow. This is a danger in places such as the Sahel in Africa, on the southern fringes of the Sahara. Trees are cut down for fuel, while goats, cattle, and other animals are allowed to eat the plants. Without protection, the topsoil blows away with the wind and the land become a desert.

GLOSSARY

Bacteria   Tiny organisms, far too small to see without a microscope. Bacteria is found just about everywhere.

Bedrock   The layer of solid rock underneath soil.

Cap rock   A layer of dense rock that traps a layer of gas or oil in the rocks below.

Compounds   Substances formed when two or more elements are joined together chemically.

Crystals   Solids with regular shapes formed by many minerals.

Decomposers   Animals, bacteria, and fungi that break down the remains of other living things.

Elements   Very simple substances that cannot be broken down by chemical means.

Erosion   The movement of fragments of weathered rock carried by wind, water, or ice.

Eruption   The sudden forcing of lava out of an opening in the earth's surface.

Extinct   No longer living or active. Used to describe a type of volcano that has not erupted for a very long time and is unlikely to do so again.

Fertilizer   Chemicals or animal waste that is added to the soil to help plants grow.

Humus   A black or dark brown substance produced by the breakdown of the remains of plants and animals in soil.

Igneous rocks   Rocks formed when magma from inside the earth cools and solidifies on the earth's surface.

Lava   Magma that has reached the surface of the earth.

Lichen   A simple type of living organism made up of a fungus and an alga living together.

Limestone   A type of sedimentary rock, often containing the remains of ancient plants and animals.

Magma   Hot, liquid rock formed deep inside the earth.

Metamorphic rocks   Rocks changed by heat or pressure inside the earth.

Minerals   Any solid elements or compounds found naturally in the earth.

Pesticides   Chemicals used to kill insects or other pests that attack crops.

Plankton   Microscopic plants and animals that drift in the sea and rivers.

Prospector   Someone who searches for valuable minerals.

Rock cycle   The continuing change of the earth's rocks from one form into another over millions of years.

Sedimentary rocks   Rocks formed from layers of the remains of older rocks that have been squeezed together.

Sediments   Loose fragments of rock deposited in one place by wind, water, or ice.

Shock waves Waves of energy that are sent out when, for example, rocks move deep under the ground. When shock waves reach the earth's surface, they make it shake.

Solution A liquid in which a solid or gas is dissolved.

Topsoil The top layer of soil, usually containing parts of dead plants and animals.

Weathering The breaking down of rocks by ice, wind, rain, or sun.

BOOKS TO READ

Asimov, Isaac. *How Did We Find Out About Volcanoes?* New York: Walker & Co., 1981.

Berger, Melvin. *As Old as the Hills.* Discovering Science. New York: Franklin Watts, 1989.

Dixon, Dougal. *The Changing Earth.* Young Geographer. New York: Thomson Learning, 1993.

Dudman, John. *Earthquake.* The Violent Earth. New York: Thomson Learning, 1993.

Farndon, John. *How the Earth Works: One Hundred Ways Parents and Kids Can Share the Secrets of the Earth.* New York: Reader's Digest Association, 1992.

Horenstein, Sidney. *Rocks Tell Stories.* Beyond Museum Walls. Brookfield, CT: Millbrook Press, 1993.

Jackson, Julia A. *Gemstones: Treasures from the Earth's Crust.* Earth Resources. Hillside, NJ: Enslow Publishers, 1989.

Kerrod, Robin. *Mineral Resources.* World's Resources. New York: Thomson Learning, 1994.

Malin, Stuart. *The Story of the Earth.* Mahwah, NJ: Troll Associates, 1991.

Oliver, Ray. *Rocks and Fossils.* New York: Random House Books for Young Readers, 1993.

Parker, Steve. *Rock and Minerals.* New York: Dorling Kindersley, 1993.

Peacock, Graham and Jesson, Jill. *Geology.* Science Activities. New York: Thomson Learning, 1995.

Stangl, Jean. *Crystals and Crystal Gardens You Can Grow.* First Books. New York: Franklin Watts, 1990.

Taylor, Paul D. *Fossil.* New York: Random House Books for Young Readers, 1990.

Watt, Fiona. *Planet Earth.* Tulsa, OK: EDC Publishing, 1991.

INDEX